# GRIEF FLOWERS

Poems By
## Megan Merchant

GLASS LYRE PRESS

Copyright © 2018 Megan Merchant
Paperback ISBN: 978-1-941783-52-8

All rights reserved: except for the purpose of quoting brief passages for review, no part of this book may be reproduced or transmitted in any form or by any means, electronic or mechanical, including photocopying, recording, or by any information storage and retrieval system, without permission in writing from the publisher.

Cover art: "Clot" © Annnmei | Dreamstime.com
Design & layout: Steven Asmussen
Copyediting: Linda E. Kim

Glass Lyre Press, LLC
P.O. Box 2693
Glenview, IL 60025
www.GlassLyrePress.com

# Contents

## I

| | |
|---|---|
| Wounds | 1 |
| How to Grow a Broken Spine | 2 |
| What I hear when the doctor says *let's have a look.* | 4 |
| Pampiniform | 5 |
| Our Fourth Try for a Second Child | 6 |
| Growing Jasmine | 8 |
| Seven Year / Flood | 9 |
| Oose | 10 |
| Holding the Mountain Together / Before You Climb | 11 |
| Scarlet Milkweed | 12 |
| How to Share Bad News | 14 |
| Long Division | 15 |

## II

| | |
|---|---|
| The Pattern of Moths | 19 |
| Tucking My Babies Into Bed | 20 |
| Yapness | 21 |
| How to Speak to Lust | 22 |

## II (Cont'd)

| | |
|---|---|
| Grief Flowers | 24 |
| Lighting a Candle for Our Dead | 25 |
| Ossuary | 26 |
| Reparations | 28 |
| Striking Distance | 29 |
| Vagitus | 32 |
| Xenoglossia | 33 |

## III

| | |
|---|---|
| Habitat for Humanity | 37 |
| Road Closure, Aleppo | 38 |
| Giving My Son the World | 41 |
| My hands | 43 |
| Dropped Stitch | 45 |
| In this dream | 46 |
| Vermeil | 48 |
| Even put back together, | 49 |
| Making Soap | 51 |
| Ghazal for Unspoken Sorrow | 52 |
| Cafuné | 53 |
| Ablepsia | 55 |
| Ianthine | 56 |
| "Song of the Lady-Axe" | 57 |
| Working the Night Shift | 59 |

| | |
|---|---|
| Acknowledgements | 63 |
| About the Author | 65 |

For my mother,
 who taught me courage & how to read the hoofbeat of wild horses.

I

# Wounds

We plant a jar of winter seeds
we spit and save

from a season of rinds
and pulp,

sow them with
just-bought packets—

Fennel, Milkweed,
Thyme—

in a window-garden
without chalking little markers
for each.

When we swell it with water
there will be shoots

from old seasons
breaking through dirt

with the same
tender-nowness.

And because we won't know
them from each other

our mouths will speak
only *bloom*.

# How to Grow a Broken Spine

He calls it/kisses it—
*the small of my back,*

the peach-soft
lean
along
my spine,

the blown-glass
curve
that cases
the filament
of spindled nerves—

how hot
the tungsten
that nearly
burns

before the
light
gleams
visible.

His hands
share the same
palm-curve,

and when pressed
firm as a book
of prayers,
holds
a gap,

a secret
crooked
under a tongue

that proves
we are each
and each
a body,

a garden
to be ironed
smooth
by rain.

When I was young
I was told
this is how
God put me
together—

sacral arc,

made to feel small
as a woodland creature
in a flood,

a hairpin turn
always leaning into dark.

# What I hear when the doctor says *let's have a look.*

I need to read you, your calligraphy of scars,
to see if our arguments with gravity are a match.

The raven gave you eyes that green.
The sparrow—a need to curtain the storm.

You are here because the wind is fleecing
the yard with cottonwood blooms. It is all right to cry.

You held a week-old hummingbird in your palm,
you can handle the quick thread of a heart,
outpacing your own.

You can handle the way that light tricks
us into thinking we are more and last.

# Pampiniform

The way he said *come here*. Kissed the tip of my shoulder.
Bare now. The dress strap slipped. Deck of cards stacked
into a pyramid on the porch table, our weathervane. No wind.

Means when the school bus groans to a three o'clock stop
in front of our house, we will hear the blur of honeybee
chatter from the windows and think wisteria.

How the botanist said the seeds will sprout, but might
never bloom. But how they vined and dipped mischievously
underground. Choked the wood post that crutches our land.
Clockwise. Rooted, breaths away from where we planted it.

(The small stone in my belly, vein-dry.)
*We'll try again.* His whisper collarbone-thin.

I grip a pad of steel wool to buff the rust spots on our shears.
Then cradle the sharp edges in soapy water, my fingers pale as milk.

I float a handful of violet clippings in a steel pot,
sprinkle soda ash, leaves and stems, soak a dress overnight,
the silk staining morning-soft—yellow bled into green.

# Our Fourth Try for a Second Child

### I.

Let us not mention the alleles
I imagined as bulb-light dripping

between trees, a cocktail party swirling
with conversation and chilled drinks,

fortune-teller at the table reading
from tea leaves and want.

Invitation by a one-in-four chance.


### II.

This gene, the specialist circles in red,
clots the birdsong

once the egg is snuggled into the nest.
Stops the heart precisely.

But not always. The odds can live
in no one's favor.


### III.

We leave and must decide
to lie down tonight with a purpose

other than letting our bodies *please*.

To know that what we create
might be kept darkly.

The God-choice—ours.


    IV.

The firing squad stands us
on the mound,

a horde of butterflies or bullets
leaving the gun-mouths,

lead and crepe-paper wings
determined to fly.

# Growing Jasmine

I root it in a clay pot
to please the gods, push a stick
into the soil,

let it vine near the light
so that it's not gorged
behind glass—how

I was taught to receive
an offering.

The window, netted with
jasmine, is a swash of white,
through summer,

blooms armed as stars.
The coming concord
of cold loosening

petals into a drip.

I tend its wild sprigs,
which means I have learned
to speak

about growth in a way that
means loss,

and know that when the sun
slips into the lip of dark
it must be kept so—

a choir of hummingbirds
cannot pray in a church
of artificial light.

# Seven Year / Flood

It is said the body replaces itself every seven years / it un-tucks its corners and flees / It is why / these monsoons / anchor their barbed teeth / into the creek bed / why the coyotes shank the quiet / with howls / why parch lisps at the first few drops / why I no longer dream her / the clot/ so blood-red / there were no other words / why my hands stopped unbuttoning the dark / signing her name in water / rocking the blank wall to sleep / Today I mourn two / the almost mother / and the lilt that gullied / un-tucked the corners and fled /

# Oose

I promise, I thought my body was made of winter.
Pinecones slapping the firm ground. The static-shush
of sleet falling hard as knuckles. Starched branches
like wires thin-poking from the mass grave of trees.
The dead piling outside in their bone tents. Shucking
fur from a rabbit's spine that first nestled like teething
beads in the coyote's jowls. They bang the windows
with tin cups, beg me to walk barefoot into the open dark,
find melt where the ground is going solid, might still
accept the tip of a shovel, dirt like dust lolling under a bed.

# Holding the Mountain Together
## / Before You Climb

I will glue the mountain cracks
with wildflowers and flayed feathers,

place my palm on the sun-stroked face
to affirm the ridge's jaw hasn't slackened.

I will learn to mimic the raven's *kraa*,
to retreat snakes back into their skins,

cake mud to seal them for another winter.
I will re-chant my grandfather's warning—

that even the most stoic crumble under enough
weight—(his lips in front of his father's gin-fist)

this wall of petroglyphs after rain
that hammered for days, keys to its decrescendo.

But you are still tucked
under a sheet of rocks, despite.

\*

Driving to the hospital, I see a woman in her bathrobe
picking Goat's Head blooms into a box of tissues,

wondering what kind of breaks their lemon color
might be holding together.

# Scarlet Milkweed

When the fever
was burning
through,

he put me into a bath
with ginger and fennel,
rubbed almond oil
on my chest
and back.

I joked—
how delicious
the glisten
of my skin.

That week
the deerflies
found a hole
in the screen door

and I had waking
dreams they were
clustering
around the silver
knives,

tangling
in my hair.

The black bands
on their wings—

a sign of sickness
that chews
through happiness,

leaves a
downy decay,
a mildew
on its walls.

He planted
a row of scarlet
milkweed
by our bedroom
window

so when the winds
arrived, I'd see
a drift of feathery
seeds spanning
out.

A wanderlust
of joy.

And when the quilt
I'd burrowed
under finally
returned
to its fold,

I sat behind
the glass

picturing
the way station of wings
that would bloom
beside
the patch of humbled
clovers.

# How to Share Bad News

I am told not to blunt the instrument,
not to muzzle it in the soft field of my mouth,
let it wind-sway and ripple,

not to wrap it in old towels so it thuds,
take it home, run a bath with lavender and rose,
then swirl the water with my trigger finger.

I am told to read the script of it verbatim,
not to trench too closely, slip
and say instead *ceased, flatlined, perished,*

because pain nuzzles into language—
hungry, suckling sleep.

I am told not to lean into it, or let it brush my skin,
because skin to skin
makes the other want to look you in the eyes,

but when my son climbs onto my lap
and needs to know the *what* and *how*—

I buck. The news has already sterilized the terror
by printing the number of bodies.

And in our house, we do not simply say *bones.*
We name them, along with each artery,
so I can teach my son how to absorb the bullets
without bleeding out.

# Long Division

I cannot skip a stone without counting,
the ripples winging and in them
the arithmetic of storms.

*

When my son was born, the doctor
counted stitches along my belly—
the handiwork of long division—

asked if I had chosen a name.

*

When he was curled like a nesting doll,
I sat up nights trying to feel his cry.

*

If I look into the scrim of dark, it is easier
to pray to silence, to understand how thoughts
are sounds swallowed in a body—

they ripple only so far.

*

One day, someone will ask my son
where he came from,

when they really want to know
about separation,

what he left behind.

He will remember the lightning bolt
that struck a perfect circle in the earth,

so close to the house that his bedsheets
smelled like a burning pile of rubber
and damp leaves—

the first time he understood
that even I could not keep him safe.

*

At school, he sits counting
the space between echo
and light,

gauging the closeness of a storm.

When it fuses into one,
he will panic and escape outside,

press his ear to the thickest tree,
hold his breath, and listen for grubs
eating into the bark—

a sound closest to a beating heart.

II

# The Pattern of Moths

When traveling, keep the moon to your left.

Prefer exposed bulbs and angora sweaters folded
in the back of a closet.

Leave all that you touch in dark; star-bitten, chewed.

Flake at a finger's brush along your wings.

Find the sweetness in rotting fruit. Eat anything
that dissolves in water.

You will know how to find the thin skin of flowers
in a storm, follow the dampened scent of honey.

Be mottled, windblown, singed by coming too close
to the light.

Congregate along doorsills, and if one opens,
flick inside.

You are a dead leaf, grains of sand,
tea-stained lace,

a crepe kite that cannot chew through wind.

# Tucking My Babies Into Bed

One child climbs into the fireplace to sleep,
 I kiss her chicory lips to ash.

In the morning, I'll scoop her into the
flower bed, bathe in the spackled light.

Another rests on the rocking chair outside.
Her gap-toothed heart is opaque as the moon
behind clouded glass.

She reads from bark resin and braids
sleeves of dried sheds, flaked bees' wings.

I bathe my twins in a spill of gas, iridescent
scalps, opal hair that tantrums
in the drooling wind.

They were here first, but only long
enough to teach me how to grieve
a clot of blood, an outline of tinsel bones,

a split, useless heart.

# Yapness

Is trying
to convince yourself

that not-having
is not-wanting,

that your bright body
is not a pen

leaked in the wash.

That you are half-supple,
and men's eyes

prim the rest.
That you don't love

the way your bones
pearl your neck,

rise under skin
as newly buried,

the cage of it
in your throat

rasps a congregation
of birds

clawing to be free.

That you don't dream
of being

light enough
to find

pelts of air
and be carried home.

# How to Speak to Lust

It tangs,
is the damp soil
under stone,

a planter bed
wisped with dill,

the way he draws
his palm along
my jaw

to explain
the language of flowers,

how bolt means
to bloom

and heat ushers
such opening,

how even a light wind
will hush
it to collapse.

It's the feathery
leaves pinched
between nails,

the yellow spindles
staining a palm,

so everything
grasped
waxes.

It is the way salt
dries—

a chalk-ring,
needing wet
to fade,

the soil
well-drained
and plotted.

It's his promise
that the leaves,
seeds & flowers
can braise
in my mouth,

the steamed chicken
with basil and mint
that aches
for a sprig
to sour

the unbearable sweetness.

# Grief Flowers

I lay my ring in the glass dish
each night to scrub my hands clean.

The band, silver, was picked knowing
it would grow soft with scratches.

My husband sets his by the bed,
brink-gray, titanium,
before reaching for my body—

a vase overfilled with grief flowers,
popping blood-red from their thin stems.

I think, if I let him
stroke me close to the catch
in my breath,

will it thrum electric to the tangle of tissue
that wadded into a clot.

Can our bodies
whisper her back into being?

I know already, if it does not pass-
slip into the toilet to be flushed,
they will lace my veins with a syringe
of dreams and clean house.

Suck the wishbone
and eyelash flutters of growth

from their nest—where she'd rather
stay, daughter of mine, marrowed
in my blood,

collapsed underneath the weight
of a name we never let fully
leave our mouths.

# Lighting a Candle for Our Dead

I hear the woodpecker's hollow knock,
but the door is sewn with weeds.

The widow's web glints mystic
in the alcove
before the house unsettles into waking.

For now, I stand a breath away
from a hummingbird on the branch

and watch how the light brightens
her feathers red
where a heart would be

if I had glued her together.

My grandmother told me
that wisp is the mouthpiece
of the dead,

flapping back.

But when I stand on the tallest table
and try, my own arms stick in the joints.

I want to know if she has nested my unborn
in this late frost,

if her knuckles still crick when held,
if her skin is still slogged over fishing-line bones.

Or, if she is able to unseam the finery of something
as lonely as prayer,

knot it around her for warmth.

# Ossuary

I dress the winter-window with plastic.
The chill vacillates between

*here* and *there*,

weeps the way a prayer
holds longing.

A strew of hawks
flock to the fence,

they drop feathers to find their way home.
Some snag the tips of branches

and prong the morning dark—a mercy,

a plea.

They have come to tell me about God,
to watch me peck at suffering,
strip my shirt,

share my ribs.

They beg to let their beaks
daub the holes this year has left

with bits of prey,

promise it will hurt only enough
to catch the scatter and fury of her pulse,

package it neatly into a bomb,

because God, they claim, is useless
without a church,

and together we shall make the tallest
out of bones,

a choir from the mass graves,
and chorus of tweets.

He will leave as many as it takes
to house an audience;

their fear will hold them quiet enough
that each breath, against his ear,

will echo applause.

# Reparations

I would quick-wrap each massacre in cellophane to clot the bleed,

mend the blood-splay of galaxy-shaped holes darted through clothes
with strips ripped from my closet of blue baby blankets.

I would sew slipcovers for knife tips—out of lamb's wool, soaked in coffee—
because that brewed smell lives in some wistful, homesick part in all of us.

I would plug the open-mouth barrels with strands of hair that birds might
otherwise gather for their nests,

untangle the church bells and scriptures, lay every letter into a wave,
let the oceans sort it out.

I would wind the naïve clock back to the crackled morning cry,
when the pinnacle of anger was being woken too early, before the sun,
by a child who wanted nothing more than to be held.

# Striking Distance

I never expected it
to be as loud—

the blinding split
that divided
the ponderosa pine
towering our roof,

the air snuffed with
its strike,

the same
smell that flooded
the surgical suite

when the specialist
sealed the curtain
of my body

after unwrapping
my son from the cord
that snared his neck.

      \*


After the storm,
I never saw an obvious
ground-scar along

that acre, if it glassed,
or veined,

nor the oviform—
purpled jellyfish,
meaty pulp of placenta,

its finery—a network
of arteries like neurons

that flicker in a brain
when someone loved
enters the room.

    *

I read that a maternity
hospital was bombed
in the Idlib Province,

and imagine mothers-in-wait
laboring in their beds
when it struck,

the contractions
not welled enough
to hold the walls
from collapsing,

and the other mothers
cradling newborns to their chests,
wondering if they

would have been safer
if birthed a few days too soon.

I imagine, just seconds
before the blast, a mother
playing at being scared,

covering her face with hands
like a shutter winking
in the wind,

her son's nerve cells,
as vast as the Milky Way,
firing when her face

appears close,
then drifts away.

# Vagitus

The first cry splits heartwood with a rusted blade.
There is a rush to suck my fluid from his lungs.

They hand him over the blue sheet,
hung so I would not see my own intestines unknotted,
laid to length, searching a tear.

My little nub-bloom—love note folded
into a white curd of cauliflower.

He roots and latches
as a growth tipped along a spring branch,
heart-flicker of a perched sparrow.

His veins, blue burrowing along his scalp,
soft spot like sun-warmed plastic covering a ditch.

I twitch with panic—a thing not meant to rise so constant—
worried that my own shadow will open and devour my young.

# Xenoglossia

First the raven, dark as oil slick on the gravel drive, clammed-beak
that would take an arrowhead tip to breach. Then feathers drifting
      in carpels of air, riding the loom of an approaching storm.

My mother's call with a premonition that the surgeon will nick
the tendriled rope of her body with his blade, and she will not
      be able to rise and clear his table.

Today, a house finch netted into the corner of the chapel,
noon-drunk, wings warping darned feathers. The wild pumping
      of its chest—arrhythmic,

as if the heart finally unhooked its corset-ribs and flooded
every nook, crushing bones like nipped shell. The second
      before stiffening, the bird curled into itself

to make a neat package of death, ready to be swept into the creek.
I was the only one who saw it clawing the smooth ground as if
      to latch or arch for something sharp to open its skin

just enough to relieve the pressure of being swallowed inside out.
It must have sensed my presence, watching over with useless hands
      while it flailed, as the heart must do before it can overwhelm
            and speak to its own living.

III

# Habitat for Humanity

I crafted walls of cellophane
to pen the light.

Added wood and slicks of plaster.
Painted every corner gray.

It became a house.

I carved a cliff and splurged
on waves to crash the dug-out rocks;

the salt-spray drew seagulls and time grew moss.
I tightened the screws to the door

so the hinge could squeak and feel authentic, aged.
And the windows, I stole from cottages once the smoke

drifted to sleep inside the mouths of chimneys
and darkness became the kind of still that wraps

around dreams. I wanted to know the view from inside
of a place called there—wanted it to be here.

But the shoes left by the door were always my own,
and as much as I smudged each fingerprint,

they still looked like clouds along the glass.
There were so many reasons to cry, the flowers wilted.

Some said there was too much salt, others bowed
their heads in pain,

sore from slugging the heft of the hammer,
wondering why every nail bent under the pressure.

# Road Closure, Aleppo

When I hear, on the radio,
that your road is closed,

I think of the desert monsoon
that razed the edges
of our highway,

the only way out—
overcome

and how, completely stuck,

I thought it looked the way
my mother did when
she tucked her lower lip

to dam
the words
that wanted to leave

but would wash out
the bridge of every conversation
she had to try politely
to cross

simply because she
was a woman,

which meant she had
lips that would riven
and silt.

But closing our road
did not mean
that fruit and meat
would rot scarce,

or hold us inside a city crumbed,
where raids shamble night
and the sky is filigreed with smoke,
not stars,

and I do not have dreams
where bullets knock
door to door
looking under beds
for my children,

wanting to gnarl their
hair with sulfured breath.

I imagine you, other mother,
who know your children
cannot swim,

but that also they cannot sleep
when the walls
are broken piano keys
thudding

and hunger is a wing
flapping
against barbed ribs,

and each lullaby is sung
under a dry tongue
waltzing inside of your mouth.

When our road closed,
the neighborhood kids
inflated rafts
to float the flood-mile
for fun

and it was lightning
that blackened the ground,
thunder that bucked against fences.

I imagine, if I could touch
your hand, we would both say
that destruction is a root of nature,

but whelmed
under our tongues—
the word that means *man*.

# Giving My Son the World

What started as a layer of sheer tissue
spindled around each rib
      grew its own heart.

The doctor said I carried high,
which meant I was terrified of how
      far he would drop.

My body—a bowl to catch the drippings,
to balance the rim of him from tipping.
      He formed fingernails

and hair, my home-grown hoarder
of bones and blood, stuffed the sac
      so I could feel

the swelling-pressure of him nip
the alcove of my throat. I took stock.
      Cleaned the last breath

of each word, taught my mouth to forget
their shapes to clear room for his.
      I hid the broken bits

so that one day I could explain the world.
How there will come a point where grief
      will stink the sheets

and after licking the windows, climb
alongside, put its hand along his thigh
      and beg heavy for sleep.

That, for me, there were days where
the burden of handing over this world
      was so heavy that I could

not bend and lift him from the floor.
That while he was reaching up,
      I was sinking deeper.

# My hands

are a comb,
a rusted birdbath,
a thistle of lavender
soothing my little one
to sleep.

My long fingers
twine a net of dark
to wrap around
his drowsy
head,

to hold him
longer.

When he
sighs and settles
his weight
I know he is thick
in dream

and the dust
on the floor
wasps into the air—
a celebration of the long-lost
come to dance.

My arms become machetes,
and mouth—

thick-pulped fruit
just pulled from its skin.

I take the waxy
rind and plug the slats
where light spiders
through

even though
the air is dry
as a lullaby of yarn

and it has not rained
for months,

I know morning
will bring the stifled

groan of thunder
rolling hungry
in his belly

my hands—a flash
of lightning without rain.

# Dropped Stitch

I am learning to knit with my hands.
There is too much hurt in this world to hold
a needle, so I let my fingers bruise and bleed
onto the wool.

I watch an online tutorial
with an elegant woman speaking French.
I do not speak French.

The measurements of each word
are not the same. Her vowels wrap around
each child, hold them safe.

The history we are patterning
has a different texture. My blanket begins
to curve like a body leaning soft

against my own. Like fear.
I tell strangers that I am making a blanket,
show them my empty hands,

the dropped stitches. I do not show them
the real one. That is for warmth.
I stand in the park flushed with ravens,

where, I am told, the most suicides are found—
something about wanting the last glimpse to be beautiful.
The junipers and ponderosa pines lean darkly.

This is not the real poem. That came to me
in a rib of sleep, and when I woke, the sound
of my child crying took its place.

# In this dream

my son is in my arms,
my son wails and thrashes
against my chest,

nipples, rouged and erect,
leak ever so thinly.

My grandmother is here.
She says

*the milk isn't enough*
*the milk isn't perfect*

and rubs drops of papery whiteness
between her thumb and fingers.
She listens for the music of it,

weak, stifled, as if someone
left strings too long in the Mojave sun.

The composer forgot to add tears, she says,
and it's true, I never cried when he was born;
there were too many clouds floating over the pain,
too much honey in the air.

She smooths her hands along thighs,
rubs knuckles like raised knots
against a washing board
to loosen grains of salt
that sigh as they fall
into a cup for tea.

*Drink,* she whispers.
*Drink from the crack.*

The paper butterflies she's painted
are clipped to the curtain;
they wrinkle softly when the window is open.

The slightest breeze
makes them believe
it's enough to fly.

# Vermeil

I look up at the dulled breast scampering in the low bush below the dining room window. A Common Rosefinch, scouting seeds, the name weighed without any delight, as stocky as a housewife. (Males carry the bright

color). Little finch, coned beak wringing the dish towel, sorting socks still damp from a broken dryer. Polishing the silver. I see her in every window, looking out. Uncombed as a thing of beauty. Red apron strings loose, eyes crimped with tired, holding a child against her chest, someone who can record the feel of her heartbeat, assure her she is living. Hungering in the dry oak. Wintering in the garden.

## Even put back together,

you can't expect
a fractured wing
to heal over
the clump of tape
and crude stick propped
outright.

You can't expect it will
eventually flap.

I believe you are doing
your best.

But if I could count
each slight as a grain
of salt and slip it into
our sheets,

between tears and sweat,

we'd be an ocean
dissolving in a drain.

Love,

it's common sense—the wing
will heal angled,
bent.

Even after slipping the stick
free,

it will fly as though splinters
are piercing each beat.

And when it catches its crude
reflection
over a water stain,

it will believe
it was the light
that captured it
all wrong.

# Making Soap

I bend to scoop white ash

from the hardwood burn—
what kept the house heated against the chill,

add it to the pot of rainwater that pooled
on the porch,

boil in fat, dripped from the bone, the meat
enough to hold my little one in sleep—

I know too well how dreams are shallowed
with hunger.

I craft a small box made of scrap wood,
found near a neighbor's build, already pierced

with nails—what could otherwise become
a boat to wing across shadows, a box to hold

stilled cicadas littered over the ground.

I layer the liquid, cover it with wax
paper—swabbed as morning light through factory

glass, and finally, pinch salt into the mold, so it will
firm enough to hold shape against skin,

my hands furiously scrubbing clean the loneliness
of each callused layer.

# Ghazal for Unspoken Sorrow

What will become of us, our son resting along the line of my hip, *hum*.
The sweet whimper-whine his breath makes, lip pressing lip, *hum*.

In our half-dark, we hush hands and mouths while he's asleep in the room,
the stretched and scarred afterbirth of my body unfolding a deep-rooted *hum*.

Thin white milk streams from my nipples onto your chest, a praise of unspoken sorrow.
My body weeps without permission, a primitive, broken *hum*.

A monk said, *you cannot know compassion until you love your own mother, absolutely.*
If I exhaled completely, I could die from such abandon, my heart shutter-stopping *hum*.

Today I light three candles, chant *Om Mani Padme Hum.*
Let compassion have the gravity of stone. *Om Mani Padme Hum.*

# Cafuné

*"The act of running one's fingers tenderly though somebody's hair."*
*(Brazilian Portuguese)*

I'll take fifteen minutes
to put on the rain
while you jazz,

hinting at the zipper-fit
of a single glass of red;

you say *love*, as in
a need, a country.

I lay a silk scarf
over the fishbowl,

watch
your hands
work the knife
through the onion, whole,
with such delicate
anger,

diced small
into tears,

but, oh, how
we open
our mouths
at the reach of each other,

pretending
we're going to pull
the cork free,

sleep with the windows
open,

be okay watching our breath
wander acres of dark
like arrows,

under clouds
that seem to have
bellied just for us,

the way, when we first met,
you paused

and came close to touching
my cheek,

saying *I like
the way you wear your hair*—
straight, damp.

Not needing
a name, or address,

but a promise—
the soft heart of bread
when it's broken,

the crust—
trailed all over the floor.

# Ablepsia

The trees cower, slant in the calling storm. We spark a fire
in case the power lines drop and our heated house chills.

I read my little one to sleep, books that ache with simplicity,
naming animals loading onto the ark—

mythologies that claim a great flood carried people
across the plains, shifted their language until they could no

longer understand those who had become others.

When the rain starts, lights flicker like an argument between
hummingbird wings and air. We are left to negotiate our way

to each other through dark—my breath, quickening, fleeing
to the roughness of his hands, where I'm still understood,

for now.

# Ianthine

Nina Simone's voice curls, a pool of fingerlings necking pockets of light. The record needle slips into a vein, swells the room, and I'm bent. The way I pointed out the doe, bounding into an open field, to my son in the back seat. As grace. As presence. When the second one is stunted mid-leap by the blue car in front of us, metal bending to its motion. Blood mixing violet into the paint. As in oncoming. As in what chases us all. *It was swift,* I console, *suffered little. Its heart stopped beating before the blood pooled.* And Nina sings. My hands, a shovel, a rake, a broom. Trying to keep the seasons from piling. Her voice like hands braiding marrow, snapping bone.

# "Song of the Lady-Axe"

*"Where are your cavils about the Soul now?"* —Walt Whitman

There is no shame in asking for the *lady axe* /
because you can't arc the heft of his

    over your head without it slamming blade-tip /
bloodying into your thigh.

    It's okay to want things lighter / —the woodpecker's
hollow hammering pulling day

    from its husk, the kale leaf—moon-large /
in its bed. Winter is just down the road

    with its single bulb and bent-light. And this year /
your son is singing where last he clamped.

    /

    It's okay to ask the man at the hardware store /
for the lightest blade. You woke this morning

    in a world where a five-year-old girl was beaten /
with a closed fist until green dripped

    from her nose and her father tried to clean her /
stilled breath with his own.

    /

    When the man doesn't want to sell you the axe /
tell him you have spent nights studying

    each split where the wood is ready to break /
by running your ungloved hand

      along its grooved wounds, that you will stow /
your weight in softwood, and that living

      tucked in these trees means you have learned to quell /
the echo and sway, to read the tracks

      and recognize that there is a soul in things, but also /
there is what we prescribe to be the soul,

      in that the grackle's call is the same timbre /
as the cringe of the rusted gate.

# Working the Night Shift

String a white sheet
from the body of trees
in the wild,

set a lantern
behind its screen
and wait

for the flush of
mottled wings
to lisp and net
the light,

note how
some are frayed
as edges of a rug
beaten against
wind,

how the brightest
markings allow
the most brazen
behavior,

a wingspan—that
if crumpled
inside a mouth—
will tart a tongue.

Wait as they collect
like silk eyes
twitching,

paper darts
that shred rain,

and can trace
the scent
of a wounded leaf
to know where
to slip their young
safely.

Wait long enough
and they will show
you how to be reborn
into night.

# Acknowledgements

A note of gratitude to the following editors and publications: *Cider Press Review*, *Comstock Review*, *Cordite Poetry Review*, *Dancing Girl Press*, *Diode*, *Glass: A Journal of Poetry*, *Eyedrum Periodically*, *Glass Lyre Press*, *Jacar Press*, *Lumina*, *Mothers Always Write*, *Mom Egg Review*, *Pittsburgh Poetry Review*, *Poets Reading The News*, *Queen of Cups*, *Rat's Ass Review*, *Rattle*, *Rise Up Review*, *Ruminate Magazine*, *The Compassion Anthology*, *The Literary Nest*, *Throwback Books*, *Tinderbox Poetry Journal*, and *3Elements Review* for first publishing versions of individual poems that appear in *Grief Flowers*.

# About the Author

**Megan Merchant** lives in the tall pines of Prescott, AZ with her husband and two children. She is the author of three full-length poetry collections with Glass Lyre Press, *Gravel Ghosts* (2016), *The Dark's Humming* (2015 Lyrebird Award Winner, 2017), *Grief Flowers* (2018), four chapbooks, and a children's book, *These Words I Shaped for You* (Philomel Books). She was awarded the 2016-2017 COG Literary Award, judged by Juan Felipe Herrera, the 14th Annual Beullah Rose Poetry Prize, and most recently, second place in the Pablo Neruda Prize for Poetry. She is an Editor at The Comstock Review and you can find her work at meganmerchant.wix.com/poet.

# Glass Lyre Press

exceptional works to replenish the spirit

Glass Lyre Press is an independent literary publisher interested in technically accomplished, stylistically distinct, and original work. Glass Lyre seeks diverse writers that possess a dynamic aesthetic and an ability to emotionally and intellectually engage a wide audience of readers.

Glass Lyre's vision is to connect the world through language and art. We hope to expand the scope of poetry and short fiction for the general reader through exceptionally well-written books, which evoke emotion, provide insight, and resonate with the human spirit.

Poetry Collections
Poetry Chapbooks
Select Short & Flash Fiction
Anthologies

www.GlassLyrePress.com

www.ingramcontent.com/pod-product-compliance
Lightning Source LLC
Chambersburg PA
CBHW030131100526
44591CB00009B/599